ANIMAL EXTINCTION AND PRESERVATION

ANIMAL BOOKS

Children's Animal Books

BABY PROFESSOR

EDUCATION KIDS

Speedy Publishing LLC
40 E. Main St. #1156
Newark, DE 19711
www.speedypublishing.com

Animals become extinct and endangered for various reasons. In this book, you will learn about how this happens as well as what you can do to prevent this from occurring.

Woolly Mammoths In The Sunset.

HOW DO THEY BECOME EXTINCT?

Animals become extinct when there are none of the species that are alive. If an animal is referred to as *"endangered"* they are at risk of becoming extinct.

There are some animals in the wild that are considered to be extinct. What this means is that the only surviving members of the species are living in captivity, similar to a zoo.

They become extinct for several different reasons. In today's world, many are endangered or extinct due to human influence. We discuss on the following pages some of the ways that animals can become extinct.

Dodo Birds In Forest.

Dinosaur at sunrise.

NATURAL INFLUENCES

Many species have become extinct during the course of history. This is the result of a natural process. They might become extinct due to changes in the climate, such as the Ice Age, a reduced food supply, competition with other species, or a combination of all of these influences.

M any natural extinctions are isolated and happen over a long period of time. However, there are some major events that might happen quickly and cause mass extinction. Probably the most well-known would be the extinction of dinosaurs, which may have been the result of a meteorite hitting the earth.

Hunter with firearm stands face to face with rhino.

HUMAN INFLUENCES

Some conservationists today are concerned that species are becoming extinct because of human interaction. This is due to the interaction of humans increasing the rate of species becoming extinct beyond what typically would occur naturally.

HUNTING

Different species of wild animals have been hunted to the point of extinction or to the point of being critically endangered. The American Bison is an example of this. Until the Europeans arrived, they were millions of bison roaming the Great Plaints in North America. Hunting became so intense that there were only a few hundred remaining once they became protected.

19th Century Poaching of Rhinoceros.

They have fortunately survived since then on ranches and farms and are no longer considered endangered.

Species living only on islands be easily be hunted to extinction. The arrival of a tribe can quickly eliminate island species.

FURS, SKINS, FEATHERS, HORNS

Other than food, they are also often hunted for certain body parts like their horns, feathers or fur. Occasionally they are the top predators and might not have a big population to begin with. They quickly can become extinct because of the hunters.

Wild animal fur skins.

The elephant has been heavily hunted in Africa for its ivory horns. Its population went from several million to only a few hundred thousand. The elephant is now protected; however, its population continues to dwindle in certain areas because of poachers.

The tiger in China is another example. It was almost hunted to extinction for its valuable fur and its bones, as well, which traditionally were used in medicine. It remains classified today as endangered.

Endemic Sumatran Tiger.

LOSS OF THEIR HABITAT

Loss of habitat is one of the biggest threats to animals in today's world. This is a result of the human expansion, especially in agriculture. When the vast areas of land are cultivated to produce food, the natural habitats are then destroyed. This can then destroy several of the life cycles required for the organisms to survive and for the biomes to thrive.

Giraffes and zebras at waterhole.

POLLUTION

Species can be killed as a result of pollution from humans. This is particularly true with fresh water biomes such as lakes and rivers. The water can be poisoned by sewage and run-off from industrial plants as well. As one species becomes affected, other ones might die off too, causing a chain reaction once the ecosystem balance is destroyed.

Pollution in the Chao Phraya River, Bangkok, Thailand.

NEWLY INTRODUCED SPECIES

Once a new animal or plant species is introduced to the ecosystem it might become invasive, and quickly overpower and kill other species. They also might destroy a dire part of the food chain and cause other species to suffer.

Lion fish, an invasive species in the Atlantic.

ENDANGERED ANIMALS

As discussed previously, animals that are in danger of becoming extinct are referred to as endangered and there are very few still surviving in the wild.

Certain species are threatened more than others. Scientists categorize the level of risk with different names in order to track the risk of the species becoming extinct.

The Amur leopard, listed as critically endangered.

They range from the most threatened referred to as *"Critically Endangered"*, the next level being *"Endangered"*, to the least threatened being *"Vulnerable"*.

Also, there are animals existing only in captivity, such as a zoo. These animals are referred to as *"extinct in the wild"*.

Pangolin, listed as critically endangered.

WHAT ANIMALS ARE MOST ENDANGERED?

These next animals are referred to as Critically Endangered.

The Black Rhinoceros lives mostly in Western Africa. There are only a few left and are mainly threatened because of hunters killing them to get their horns.

The Red Wolf originally roamed the Southeast United States. There are merely a few hundred left, and most of them live in captivity.

Red Wolf

Some of the other animals include the Giant Ibis, the California Condor, the Mountain Gorilla, the Florida Panther and the Siberian Tiger.

Some of the animals on the *"endangered"* list are the Snow Leopard, the Albatross, the Blue Whale, the Giant Panda, the Loggerhead Sea Turtle and the Sea Otter.

Some of the animals on the *"vulnerable"* list include the Humpback Whale, Polar Bear, Dingo, Hippo, Cheetah, Lion, and the Royal and Macaroni Penguins.

Javan Rhinoceros.

Snow leopard posing in the snowy outdoors

HOW DO WE PROTECT THEM?

Several countries around the world have enacted laws protecting endangered species. Often, it is considered a criminal act to injure or kill an endangered or protected animal. There are several laws in the United States protecting these precious animals. These are part of the Endangered Species Act that was signed by President Nixon in 1973.

The laws are in force to protect these animals as well as their habitats. There are also programs known as Recovery Plans to help animals to recover. The National Oceanic and Atmospheric Administration and the United States Fish and Wildlife Services are the main agencies enforcing these laws and helping to protect the animals.

Two panda bears in bamboo forest.

CONSERVATION OF WILDLIFE

PROTECTING ANIMALS IN NATIONAL PARKS

One major way that our government can help in conserving wildlife is by helping to protect their habitats. Many governments have created national parks where activities such as fishing, farming, mining and hunting are illegal. Development is typically prevented or limited most of the time in these areas.

BREEDING IN CAPTIVITY

Sometimes its habitat may have been destroyed and they no longer can survive in the wild. Zoos have sometimes maintained the animals and helped them develop their population in captivity.

Baby rhinoceros close-up during a safari in South Africa.

The Arabian Oryx is a perfect example. They were almost extinct due to being hunted in the early 1970s. Zoos managed to save the last few and it was declared to be extinct in the wild. Because of the captive breeding programs of the zoos, they were able to increase the population and some were then released back into the wild. The Arabian Oryx was the first species to be moved successfully from the *"extinct in the wild"* category to the *"vulnerable"* category in 2011.

Arabian Oryx.

ANIMAL POPULATIONS

One intricate part of protecting the animals involves maintaining a record of their populations. These records help scientists to understand whether the population is shrinking or growing. They use several methods to understand their population.

One method scientists use in tracking populations is having several people survey an area and check out any physical evidence including dens or burrows, animal tracks and breeding sites. While this method may take a lot of resources such as time and people, it may be the only option available. Trying to track animals such as rhinos or tigers can also be dangerous.

Tagging them with transmitters is another way to track them. The scientists can then track their movements as well as their migration patterns. Because of modern technology these transmitters are smaller and more intelligent.

Adult tagged Mountain Goat.

They can also be tracked using remote control cameras. These cameras are enclosed in a weatherproof case and often are attached to a tree located near a wildlife trail or feeding site. They utilize motion sensors which take pictures as the animals walk by.

Atlantic Puffin on rock, tagged with tracking bands.

LAWS PROTECTING ANIMALS

Making it illegal to harm or kill an endangered species is another way the government can protect animals. There are several laws as well as international treaties in force to protect animals. Anyone that kills or injures one can go to jail for a long period of time and pay a hefty fine as well. Unfortunately, some countries still have not signed the treaties or don't enforce the laws.

There are too many animals that are extinct, endangered, or vulnerable. For more information about what you can to help save them you can go to your local library, research the internet, and ask questions of your teachers, family and friends.

Visit
BABY PROFESSOR
EDUCATION KIDS
www.BabyProfessorBooks.com
to download Free Baby Professor eBooks and view
our catalog of new and exciting Children's Books